Murphy and his Friends Learn their Colors

Written by Cynthia Scott Griffin
Illustrated by Megan Dodge Sergi

Murphy and His Friends Learn their Colors
All Rights Reserved.
Copyright © 2017 Cynthia Scott Griffin and Megan Dodge Sergi
v3.0

Cover and interior images courtesy of Megan Dodge Sergi © 2017. All rights reserved - used with permission.

Griffin Publishing

ISBN: 978-0-578-18574-3

Library of Congress Control Number: 2016914848

PRINTED IN THE UNITED STATES OF AMERICA

Murphy the magnificent moose munching his ORANGE marmalade.

Richard the relaxed raccoon in his RED robe.

Yves the yodeling yak yelling from his YELLOW yacht.

Georganna the gentle giraffe gardening in her GREENhouse.

Ursula the unique unicorn under her BLUE umbrella.

Ingrid the irritated iguana ignoring INDIGO insects.

Victoria the vain vixen playing her VIOLET victrola.

William the wandering whale waving his WHITE wand.

Benjamin the baby bulldog biting his BROWN ball.

Zola the zesty zebra zipping her BLACK coat.